WEEKLY WR READER
EARLY LEARNING LIBRARY

Animals That Live in the Mountains

Bighorn Sheep

by JoAnn Early Macken

Reading consultant: Susan Nations, M.Ed.,
author/literacy coach/
consultant in literacy development

Please visit our web site at: www.earlyliteracy.cc
For a free color catalog describing Weekly Reader® Early Learning Library's list of high-quality books, call 1-877-445-5824 (USA) or 1-800-387-3178 (Canada).
Weekly Reader® Early Learning Library's fax: (414) 336-0164.

Library of Congress Cataloging-in-Publication Data

Macken, JoAnn Early, 1953-
Bighorn sheep / by JoAnn Early Macken.
p. cm. — (Animals that live in the mountains)
Includes bibliographical references and index.
ISBN 0-8368-6315-1 (lib. bdg.)
ISBN 0-8368-6322-4 (softcover)
1. Bighorn sheep—Juvenile literature. I. Title.
QL737.U53M215 2006
599.649'7—dc22 2005027919

This edition first published in 2006 by
Weekly Reader® Early Learning Library
A Member of the WRC Media Family of Companies
330 West Olive Street, Suite 100
Milwaukee, WI 53212 USA

Managing editor: Valerie J. Weber
Art direction: Tammy West
Cover design and page layout: Kami Strunsee
Picture research: Diane Laska-Swanke

Picture credits: Cover, pp. 7, 15, 19, 21 © Tom and Pat Leeson; p. 5 © Alan & Sandy Carey; pp. 9, 11, 13, 17 © Michael H. Francis

Printed in the United States of America

1 2 3 4 5 6 7 8 9 10 09 08 07 06

Note to Educators and Parents

Reading is such an exciting adventure for young children! They are beginning to integrate their oral language skills with written language. To encourage children along the path to early literacy, books must be colorful, engaging, and interesting; they should invite the young reader to explore both the print and the pictures.

Animals That Live in the Mountains is a new series designed to help children read about creatures that make their homes in high places. Each book describes a different mountain animal's life cycle, behavior, and habitat.

Each book is specially designed to support the young reader in the reading process. The familiar topics are appealing to young children and invite them to read – and reread – again and again. The full-color photographs and enhanced text further support the student during the reading process.

In addition to serving as wonderful picture books in schools, libraries, homes, and other places where children learn to love reading, these books are specifically intended to be read within an instructional guided reading group. This small group setting allows beginning readers to work with a fluent adult model as they make meaning from the text. After children develop fluency with the text and content, the book can be read independently. Children and adults alike will find these books supportive, engaging, and fun!

– Susan Nations, M.Ed., author, literacy coach,
and consultant in literacy development

A bighorn sheep can stand soon after it is born. A baby, or **lamb**, can walk in a few hours. Soon it can run and jump. A female sheep, or **ewe**, feeds her lamb milk.

In a few months, lambs eat grass. Sheep swallow their food in quick bites. Later, they bring it up to chew it. Then they swallow it again.

Ewes and lambs stay in a group. Lambs play with each other. Males, or **rams**, also stay in a group. One sheep watches out for danger.

Bighorns can see far away. If a ewe sees danger, she stamps her foot. If a ram sees danger, he snorts. The group runs down the mountain.

Bighorns are good at climbing. Their feet do not slip. Sheep leap from rock to rock. They jump off high cliffs!

A bighorn sheep's horns keep growing. A ram's horns grow back and down. They can curl into circles.

ram
ewe

Rams fight with their horns. Crash! They slam into each other!

In winter, snow can cover the grass. Sheep scrape away the snow. A group may move to a place with less snow.

Bighorns grow heavy coats for winter. In spring, they **shed**, or lose, some hair. They look for green grass to eat.

Glossary

cliffs — steep rock faces

danger — a thing that may cause harm or pain

scrape — to scratch or rub with something sharp

snorts — makes a sound by blowing air out through the nose

swallow — to pass through the mouth to the stomach while eating

For More Information

Books

The Battling Bighorns. Animal Odysseys (series). Lynn M. Stone (Rourke)

Bighorn Sheep. Aaron Frisch (Smart Apple Media)

The Bighorn Sheep. Wildlife of North America (series). Joanne Mattern (Capstone)

Trails Above the Tree Line: A Story of a Rocky Mountain Meadow. Audrey Fraggalosch (Soundprints)

Web Sites

Big Horn Sheep
www.nature.ca/notebooks/english/bighorn.htm
Illustration and facts about bighorn sheep

Index

About the Author

JoAnn Early Macken is the author of two rhyming picture books, ***Sing-Along Song*** and ***Cats on Judy***, and more than eighty nonfiction books for children. Her poems have appeared in several children's magazines. A graduate of the M.F.A. in Writing for Children and Young Adults Program at Vermont College, she lives in Wisconsin with her husband and their two sons.